Cool Science Experiments for Kids

Science and Nature for Kids

BABY PROFESSOR

EDUCATION KIDS

Speedy Publishing LLC
40 E. Main St. #1156
Newark, DE 19711
www.speedypublishing.com

This is a great way for kids to enjoy, explore and experiment, key elements of early science, while having fun!

What Colors Absorb More Heat?

Materials Needed:

- 2 drinking glasses or containers
- Water
- Thermometer
- 2 elastic bands / rubber bands
- White paper
- Black paper

What To Do:

1. Wrap the white paper around on one of the glasses using an elastic band to hold it in place.
2. Do the same with the black paper around the other glass.
3. Fill the glasses with same amount of water, at the same temperature. Record the starting temperature.
4. Leave the glasses out in direct sunlight for two hours before measuring the temperature of the water in each glass.
5. Compare each new temperature with the starting temperature.

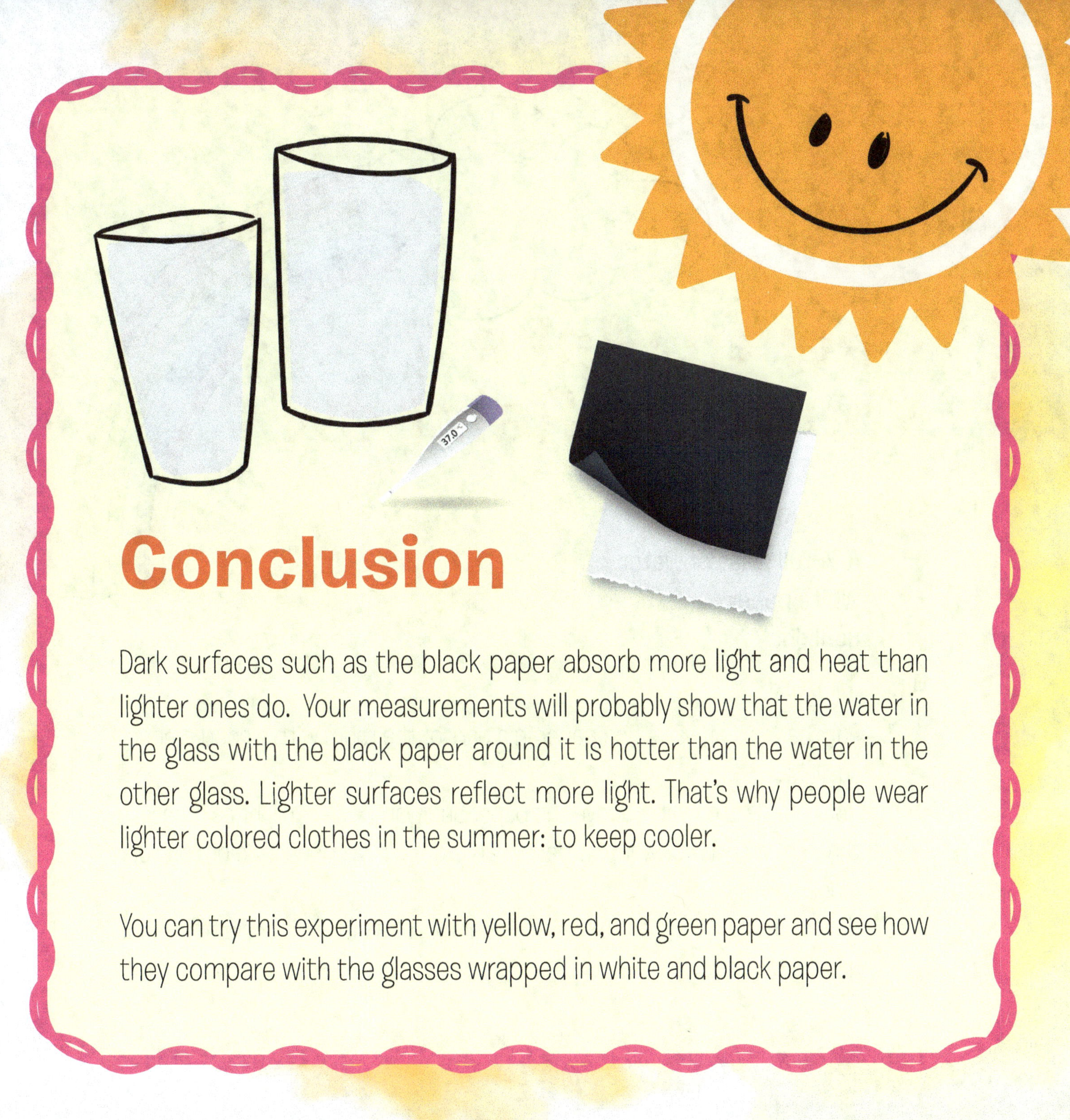

Conclusion

Dark surfaces such as the black paper absorb more light and heat than lighter ones do. Your measurements will probably show that the water in the glass with the black paper around it is hotter than the water in the other glass. Lighter surfaces reflect more light. That's why people wear lighter colored clothes in the summer: to keep cooler.

You can try this experiment with yellow, red, and green paper and see how they compare with the glasses wrapped in white and black paper.

How to Make Your Own Rainbow

Materials needed:

- A ¾-full glass of water
- White paper
- Sunlight

What To Do:

1. Put the glass of water and paper in a part of the room with a good amount sunlight.
2. Hold the glass of water above the paper and watch the sunlight as it passes through the glass of water, it bends and forms a rainbow of colors on your piece of paper.
3. Now try holding the glass of water higher and at a different angle to see if it has a different effect.

Conclusion

You may have seen a rainbow in the sky or in the mist of a waterfall, but you can even make your own as you did in this experiment.

Rainbows are formed in the sky when sunlight passes through raindrops, The effect is the same as the sunlight passes through a glass of water. The sunlight refracts, separating into different colors such as red, orange, yellow, green, blue, indigo and violet.

How to make a Crystal Snowflake!

Learn how to make a snowflake using borax and few common items found in your household. Find out how crystals are formed in this fun activity, experiment with food coloring to make crystal snowflakes as a great-looking decoration!

Materials Needed:

- String
- Wide mouthed glass jar
- White pipe cleaners
- Food coloring (blue)
- Boiling water (may need an adult to help)
- Wooden rod or a pencil
- Borax

What To Do:

1. Cut the white pipe cleaner into three sections of the same size. Twist these sections together in the center to form a 6-pointed star. Make sure that your ends are of the same length.
2. Take the top of one of the pipe cleaners and attach a piece of string to it. Tie the opposite end of the string to your wooden rod or pencil. Use this to hang your completed snowflake.
3. With adult supervision, carefully fill the jar with boiling water.
4. Add three (3) tablespoons of borax for each cup of water. Stir until the mixture is dissolved.
5. Add some food coloring if you'd like to give your snowflake a nice bluish look.
6. Put the pipe cleaner snowflake into the jar with the small wooden rod or pencil resting on the edge of the jar and the snowflake soaking completely in the borax solution.
7. Leave the snowflake overnight. Check in the morning: your snowflake is covered with crystals!
8. Hang it somewhere in your house.

FOOD COLOR
BORAX

Conclusion

Crystals consist of molecules that are arranged in a repeating pattern that extends in all three dimensions. Borax, sodium borate, it is a white powder made up of colorless crystals that can be easily dissolved in water.

When you add borax to the boiling water, warmer water molecules move around faster and are spread apart, allowing sufficient room for borax crystals to dissolve.

When the solution cools, the water molecules move closer to each other and can't hold much of the borax solution. Crystals begin to form on top of each other and before you know it you have completed a crystal snowflake!

HOW TO MAKE A BALLOON ROCKET

Materials Needed:

- 1 balloon
- 10 – 15 feet of kite string
- 1 plastic straw
- tape

What To Do

1. Tie one end of the string to a chair, table, door knob or other support.
2. Put one end of the string through the straw.
3. Pull the string and tie it to another support available.
4. Blow up the balloon. Pinch the end of the balloon and tape it to the straw.
5. Let go and watch your rocket fly along the string!

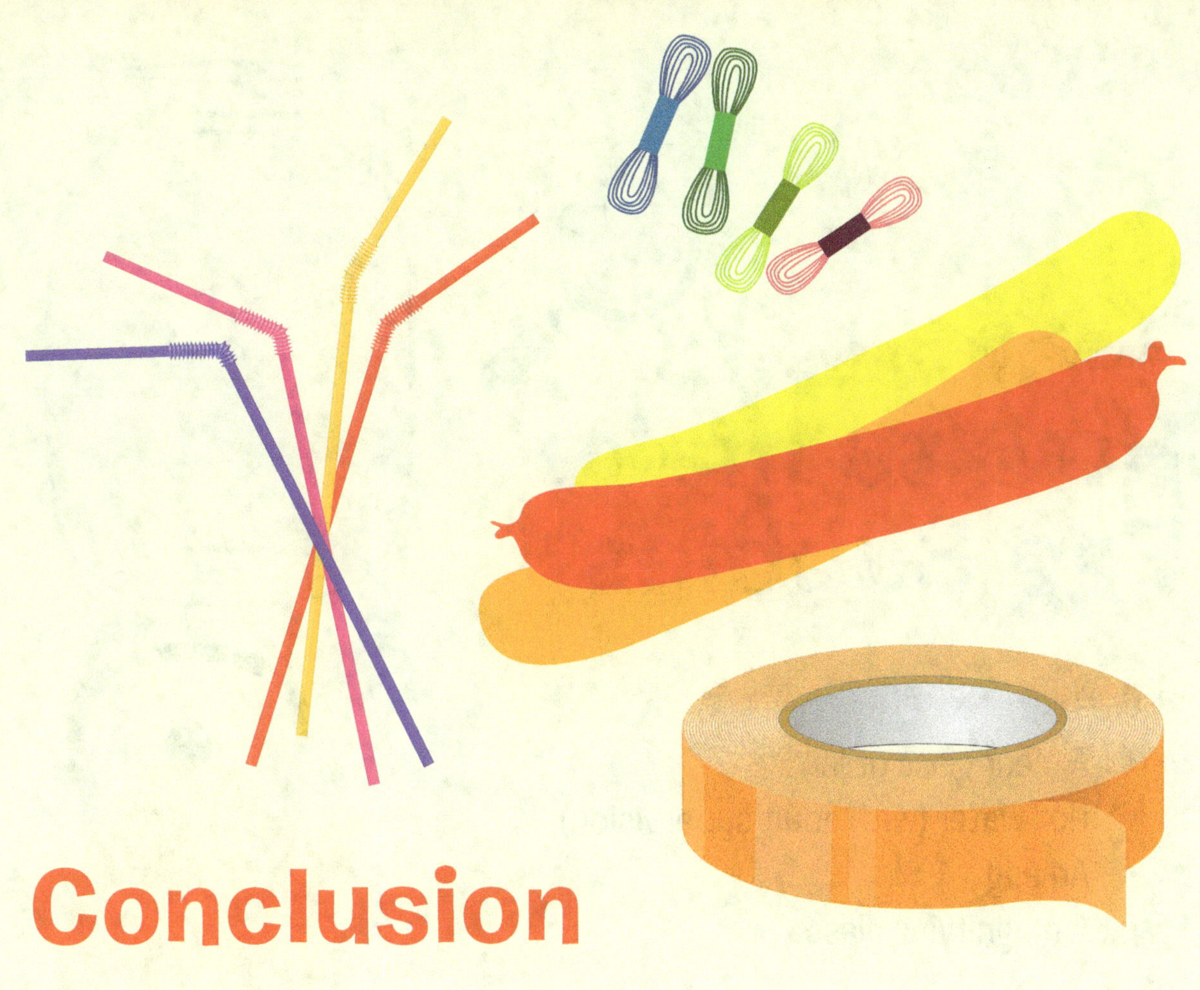

Conclusion

It's all about air pressure and thrust. As the air goes out of the balloon, it generates a forward motion called thrust. Thrust is a force created by energy. In the experiment, thrust comes from the energy of the balloon forcing the air to come out.

How to make Egg Bubbles

Materials Needed:

- A clear glass or jar
- Hot water (with adult supervision)
- An egg
- A magnifying glass

What To Do:

1. Carefully place the egg inside the glass or jar, without cracking it.
2. Carefully pour hot water into the glass until it is nearly full.
3. Put the glass on a table and watch the egg closely for a few minutes
4. Use a magnifying glass to closely examine what is happening.

Conclusion

After putting the egg with hot water you will notice small bubbles formed on the egg shell. They will eventually bubble their way up to the surface.

An egg contains small air pockets at its larger end between the shell and egg white. When the air is trapped inside these small pockets it begins to heat up and expands and finds a way out of the shell, but how does it escape?

They're too small to be seen with our naked eyes, but with the use of a magnifying glass you will be able to see that egg shells have thousands of small holes called pores.

These pores act as a passage as the air passes through the shell, making it look like the egg breathes as the air expands and is forced through the shell.

Blowing Up Balloons With Carbon Dioxide

Materials Needed:

- Balloon
- 40 ml of water
- Soft drink bottle
- Drinking straw
- Lemon juice
- 1 teaspoon of baking soda

What To Do:

1. Stretch out the balloon to make it ready to inflate.
2. Pour the 40 ml water into the soft drink bottle.
3. Add a teaspoon of baking soda to the bottle and stir with the straw until it has dissolved.
4. Pour the lemon juice and quickly put the balloon over the mouth of the bottle.

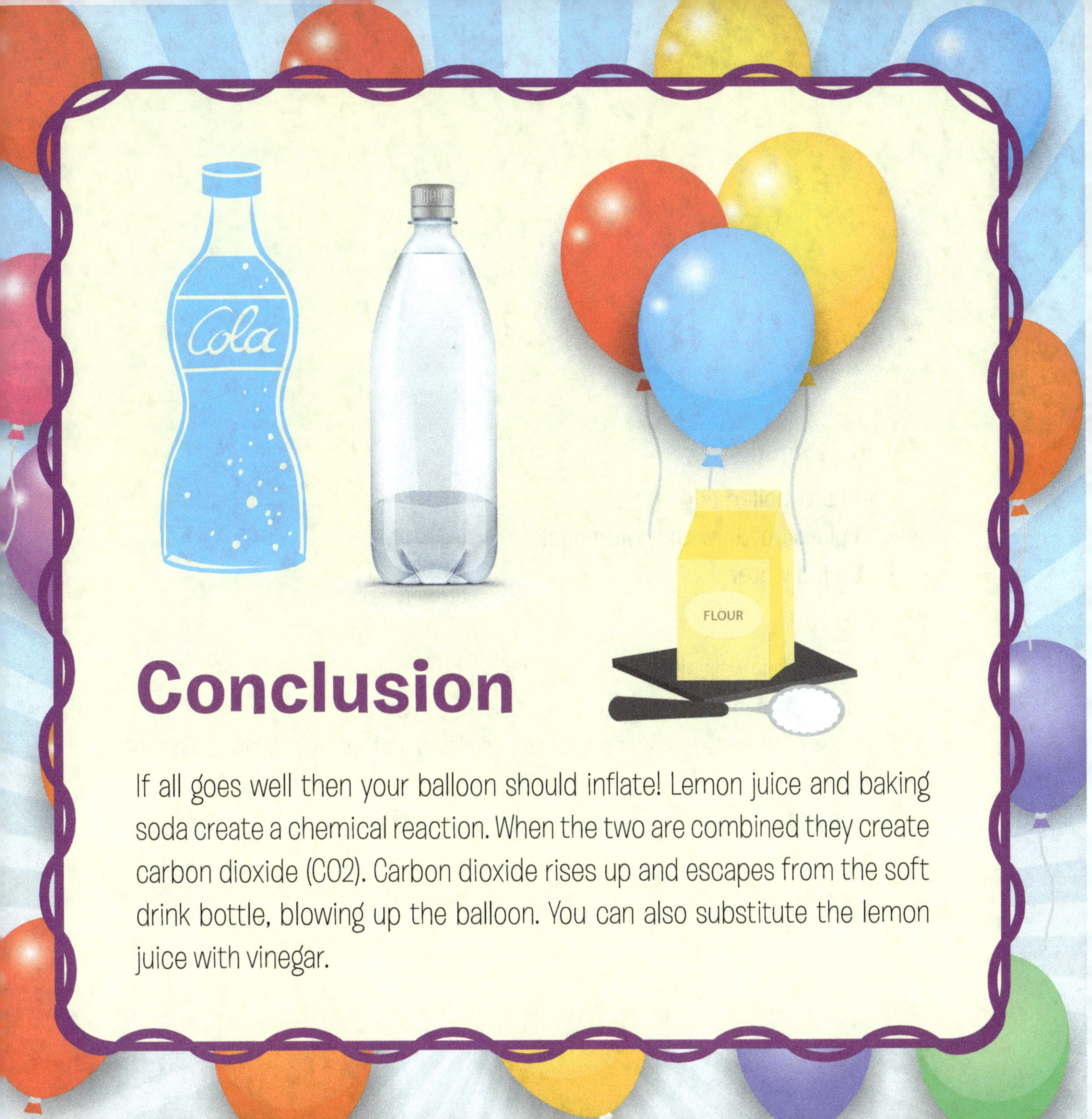

Conclusion

If all goes well then your balloon should inflate! Lemon juice and baking soda create a chemical reaction. When the two are combined they create carbon dioxide (CO_2). Carbon dioxide rises up and escapes from the soft drink bottle, blowing up the balloon. You can also substitute the lemon juice with vinegar.

Egg in a Bottle

Materials Needed:

- 1 hard-boiled egg
- 1 glass bottle with a wide neck
- Boiled water

What to Do:

1. Pour boiling water into the bottle to about a ¾ full.
2. Place the hard-boiled egg on the mouth of the bottle.
3. Watch and wait. You will notice the egg slowly shifted by the hot air in the bottle, this is when the hot air expands and escapes out of the bottle.
4. The egg will eventually get sucked inside the bottle.

Conclusion

The hot air expands and forces its way out of the bottle, making the egg shift and move up a bit.

As the air cools inside the bottle the air contracts and takes up less room and space. This creates lower pressure inside the bottle. The greater pressure outside the bottle forces the egg into the bottle.

Floating Egg

Materials Needed:

- One egg
- Water
- 1-2 cups salt
- Drinking glass (tall)
- Spoon

What To Do:

1. Fill the glass half full with water
2. Place the egg inside the glass of water and see if it sinks.
3. Add 1 tablespoon of salt and stir it until the salt dissolves. Add more salt until the egg floats.
4. Next, carefully add fresh water until the glass is nearly full. Do not mix the salty water with the plain water. You can get the egg to float between the fresh and salt water.

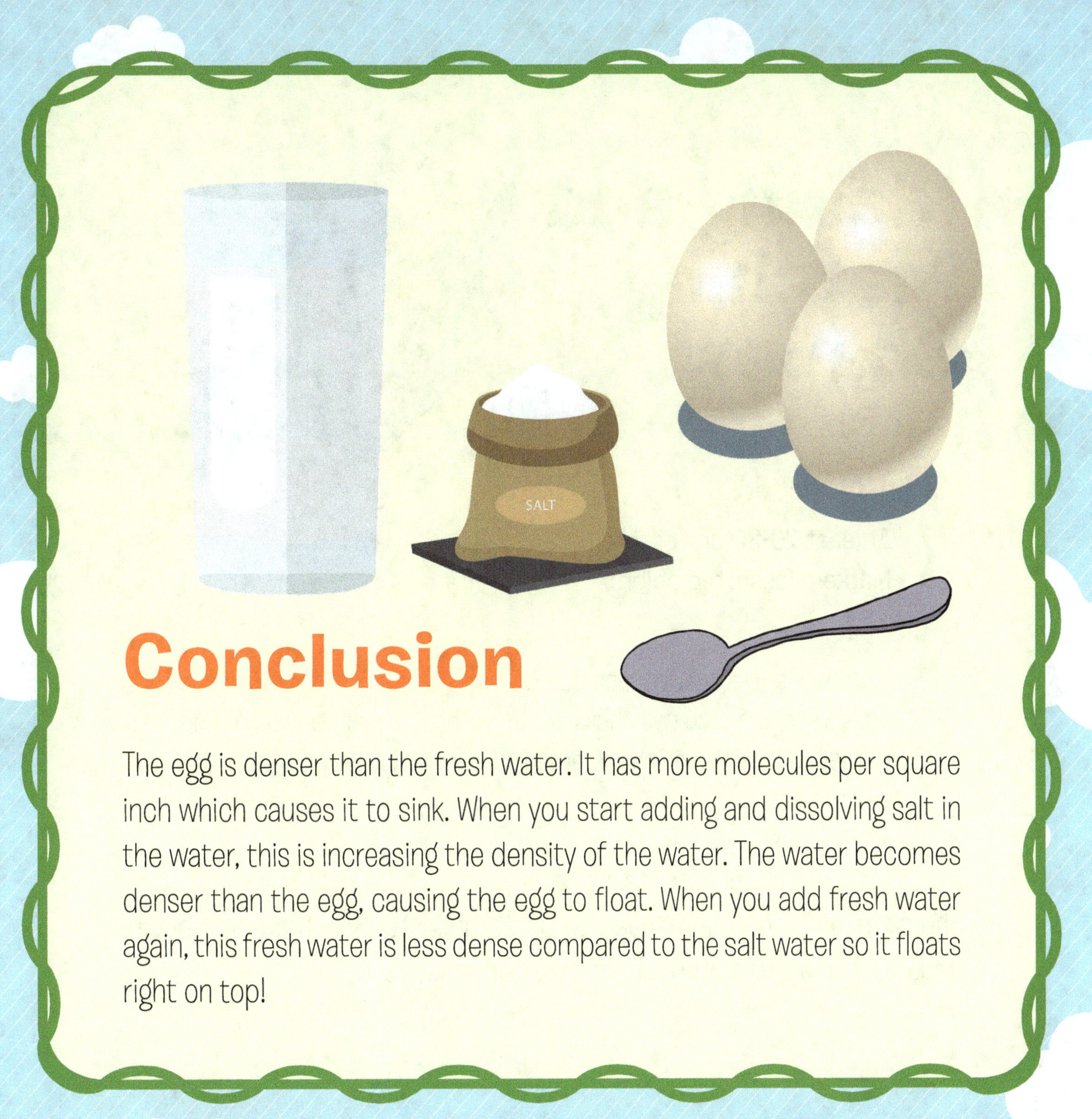

Conclusion

The egg is denser than the fresh water. It has more molecules per square inch which causes it to sink. When you start adding and dissolving salt in the water, this is increasing the density of the water. The water becomes denser than the egg, causing the egg to float. When you add fresh water again, this fresh water is less dense compared to the salt water so it floats right on top!

Making and Matching Shapes

Materials Needed:

- At least 20-30 craft sticks
- Markers (assorted colors)

What To Do:

1. Place two sticks next to each other.
2. Draw a shape on the two sticks. Split the shape equally between the sticks.
3. Repeat step 2 until you have created as many shapes overlapping stick pairs as you want.
4. Mix up the sticks.
5. Match the sticks to create shapes.

The shapes you use don't need to be complicated. Try drawing a circle, square, triangle, and other shapes that are easy to do.

How to make a Parachute Toy

Materials Needed:

- String
- Handkerchief or small piece of cloth
- Button with four holes
- Pipe cleaner
- Small stone
- Toy or an action figure

What To Do:

1. Cut four pieces of string, each one 18 inches in length. Put each string through a separate hole in the button, and tie them together, leaving a few inches of string below the button.
2. Lay out your handkerchief or cloth and stretch the other ends of the strings. Tape one string to each corner of the cloth. Now, you've got a parachute!
3. Attach an action figure or toy below the button, using the short ends of the strings.
4. Throw the action figure and parachute into the air and see what happens.

Magic Ice

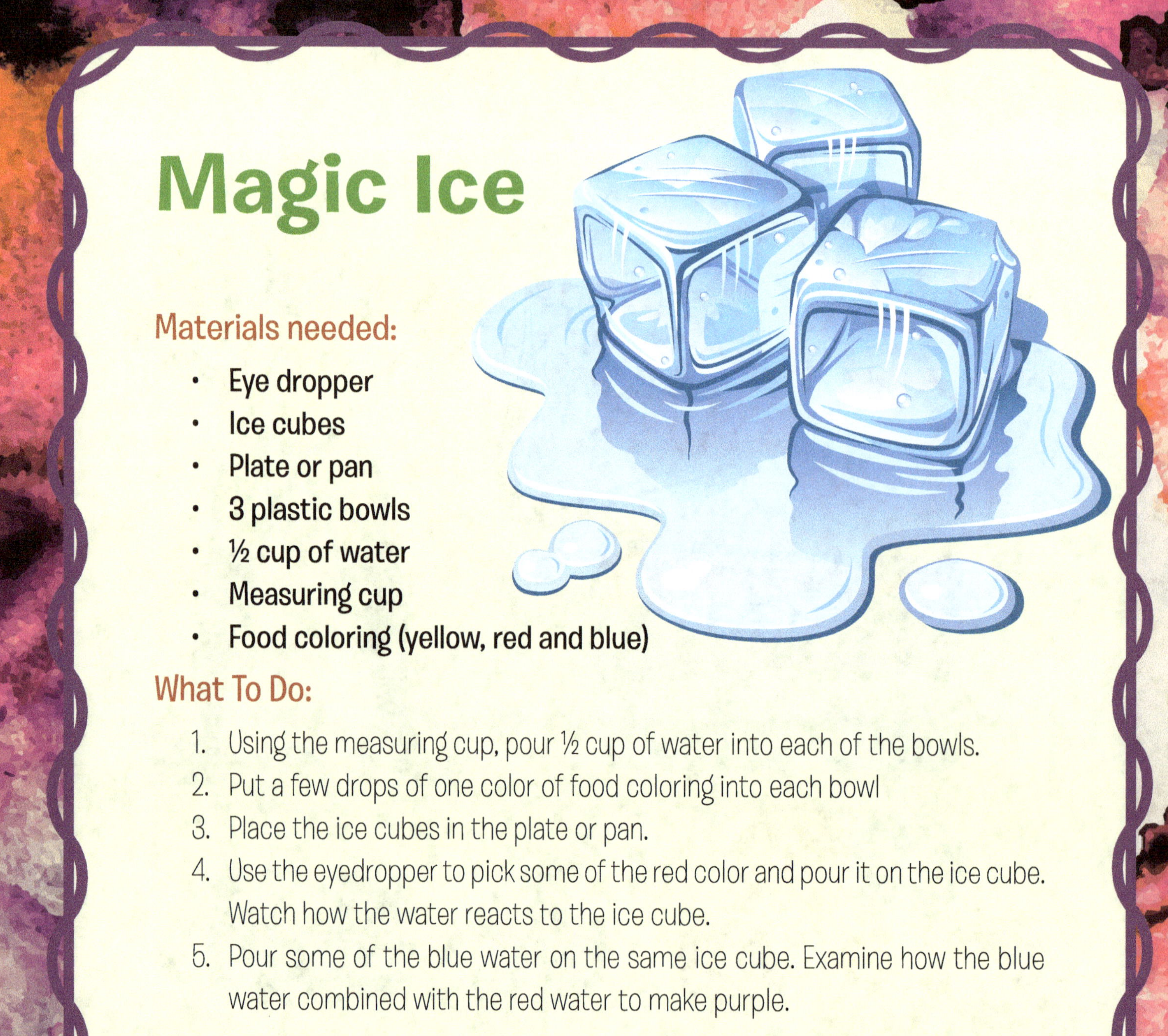

Materials needed:

- Eye dropper
- Ice cubes
- Plate or pan
- 3 plastic bowls
- ½ cup of water
- Measuring cup
- Food coloring (yellow, red and blue)

What To Do:

1. Using the measuring cup, pour ½ cup of water into each of the bowls.
2. Put a few drops of one color of food coloring into each bowl
3. Place the ice cubes in the plate or pan.
4. Use the eyedropper to pick some of the red color and pour it on the ice cube. Watch how the water reacts to the ice cube.
5. Pour some of the blue water on the same ice cube. Examine how the blue water combined with the red water to make purple.

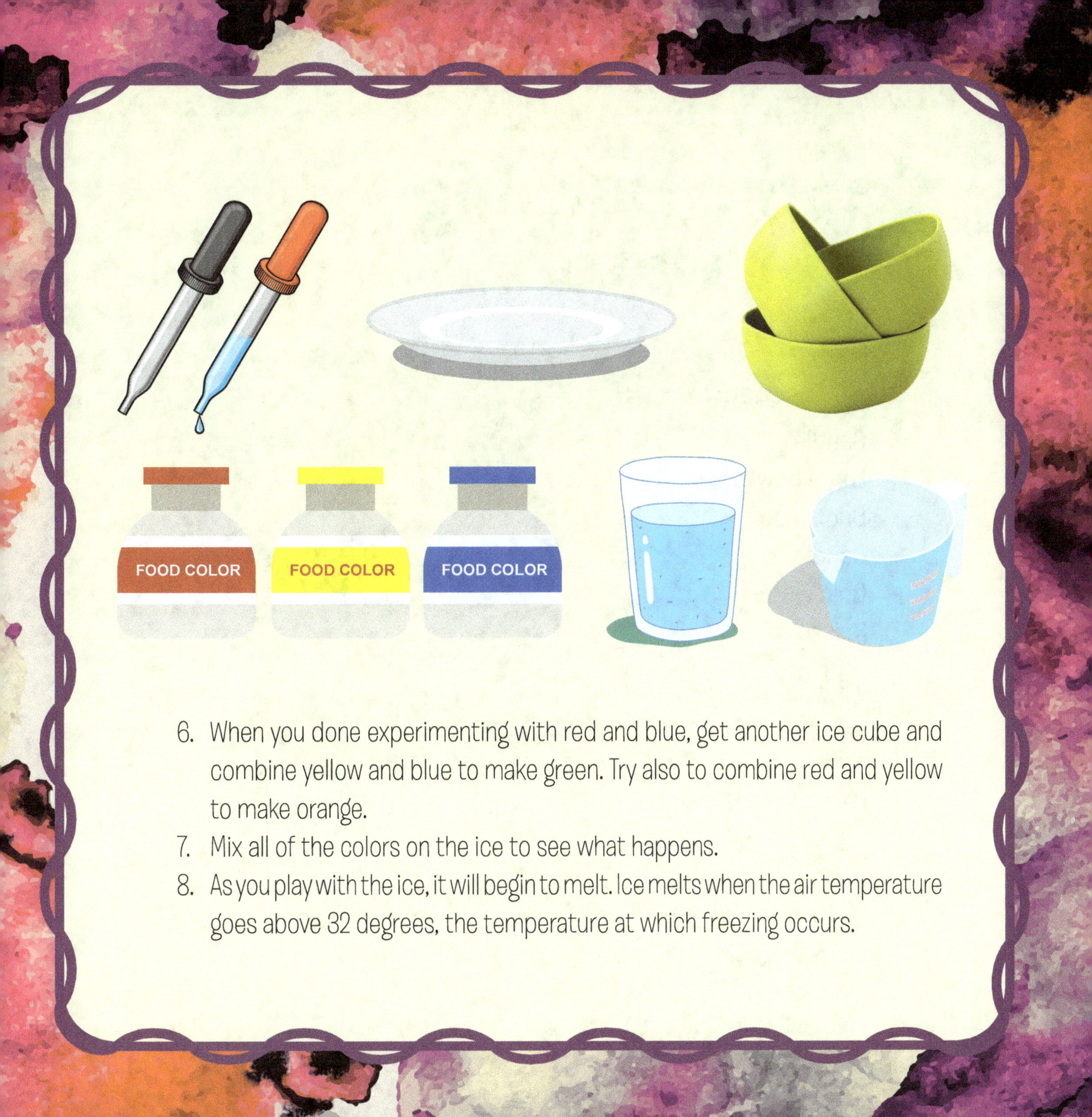

6. When you done experimenting with red and blue, get another ice cube and combine yellow and blue to make green. Try also to combine red and yellow to make orange.
7. Mix all of the colors on the ice to see what happens.
8. As you play with the ice, it will begin to melt. Ice melts when the air temperature goes above 32 degrees, the temperature at which freezing occurs.

Candle Burning Underwater

Materials needed:

- Candle
- Large bowl
- Duct tape
- Candle
- Cold water
- Scissors

What To Do:

1. Cut off four 4-inch lengths of duct tape.
2. Tape the candle to the bottom of the bowl with the duct tape.
3. Carefully fill the bowl with water just to the top of the candle. Do not submerge the wick!
4. Carefully light the candle (with adult supervision)
5. Observe what happens. The candle should burn all the way to the bottom of the bowl, leaving a thin tube of wax.

Conclusion

If you had lit the candle in a bowl without water, it would have burned normally and consumed the whole candle. This is caused by the action of both heat flow and a high temperature.

Homemade Modeling Clay

Materials Needed:

- 1 red beet (½ cup onion skins also create natural dyes)
- 1 cup water
- Strainer
- 1 cup of flour
- ½ cup of salt
- 1 tablespoon of cream of tartar
- 1 tablespoon of vegetable oil
- Small saucepan
- Medium saucepan
- Rubber spatula

What To Do:

1. Simmer 1 cup of water over medium heat. Cut and dice a small red beet and add it to the hot water. Many dark colored fruits and vegetables can create a vibrant natural dye. You can experiment with blueberries, onion skins, or any vegetables of a dark color to create several colors of modeling clay!

2. Let the water boil for 20 minutes and watch as the water turns to a deep red.

3. Pour the red water into the medium saucepan (with adult supervision).

4. Mix the flour, salt, cream of tartar, and oil in the saucepan along with the red water. Use a rubber spatula to mix them together.

5. Turn the heat to medium and keep stirring gently. Wait for the mixture to thicken and resemble modeling clay!

6. Put the hot mixture on a lightly floured surface and allow it to cool. Now you are ready to enjoy squishing and squeezing your colorful creation!

Glowing Water

Materials Needed:

- Yellow highlighter pen
- Black light or UV light
- Pair of gloves
- Glass container
- Water

What To Do:

1. Remove the back of a highlighter pen, or if this is not possible, have an adult cut the pen in half with a sharp knife.
2. Pour some tap water into a glass or container.
3. Wear a pair of gloves when pulling out the ink-soaked felt that is inside the cut pen. The gloves will protect your fingers from being stained with the fluorescent dye.
4. For an hour or so, soak the felt in a container with water. Wearing a pair of gloves, carefully squeeze the felt until all the ink has been transferred to the water.

5. Turn the black light on and watch your water glow an eerie green.
6. Use the water to transfer the glow to any water based experiments, like making slime, ice or bubbles. Tonic water also glows under UV light, so it is great to use in edible glow experiments, like making glowing jelly.

Conclusion

Tonic water and highlighters glow under UV or black light because they contain fluorescent chemicals. These chemicals absorb and then release light back. In this case they absorb highly energetic UV light that is invisible and release less energetic, visible light. The water is transparent so it is easy to color with these glowing chemical forms. The glowing water can be used again and again and never loses its glow.

HOW TO MAKE A HOT AIR BALLOON

Materials Needed:

- Dry cleaning plastic bag
- Hair dryer

What To Do:

1. Open the plastic bag and fill it with air by quickly pulling it through the air around you.
2. Close the bag with your hand, however leave a small opening.
3. Carefully insert the nozzle of the hair dryer through the opening
4. Using the hair dryer, heat the air in the bag for a few minutes
5. 5. Observe as the bag rises.

Conclusion

The molecules the air it is made up of spread out as air is warmed. This makes the air lighter, and it rises. The bag expands and rises as the air in it is warmed. Now you and your friends can start making hot air balloons.

How to Make Rock Candy Crystals

Materials Needed

- 1 piece of cotton string at least 15 cm long.
- Pencil
- Paper clip (or large plastic bead)
- 1 cup of water
- 2 cups sugar
- Glass jar

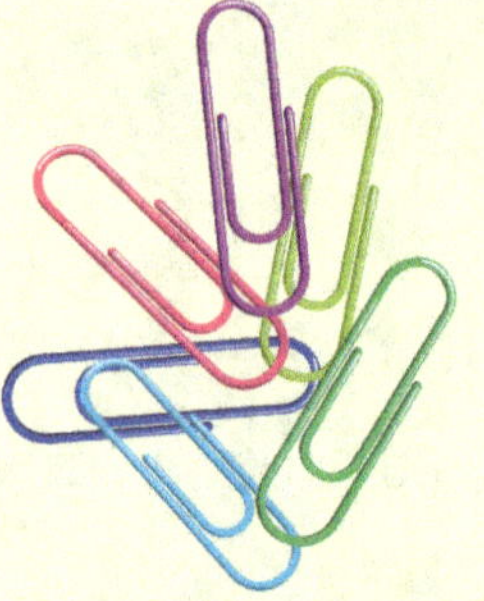

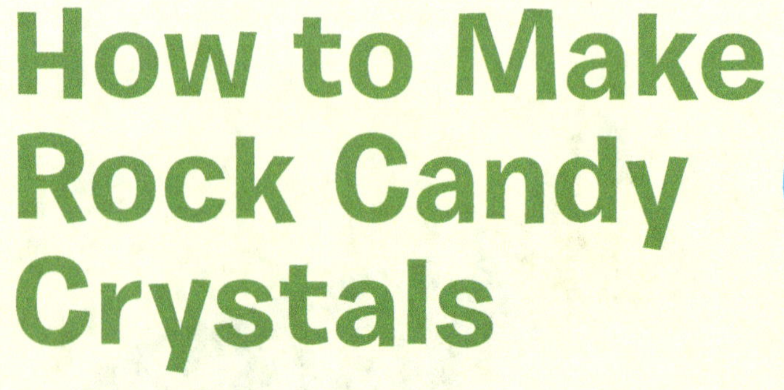

What To Do:

1. Tie a 15 cm piece of cotton string to the middle of the pencil.
2. Wet the string and roll it in sugar. Then allow this to dry.
3. Tie a paper clip to the end of the string.
4. Put the pencil at the top of the jar so that the string will hang down to the middle of the jar. If it hangs down too low, roll the string round the pencil until the string is no longer touching the sides or bottom of the jar. The string will serve as a seed for the crystal. Any type of jar will do, however pint size canning jars are especially nice, as they can endure the hot temperatures. Tall skinny olive jars are also good because they don't use up so much liquid.
5. Remove the string and pencil from the jar once they are ready and put them aside.
6. Ask an adult to help out!
7. Pour some water into a pan and bring it to a boil.
8. Put 1/4 cup of sugar in the boiling water, and stir constantly until it dissolves.
9. Add sugar little by little, and continue stirring until all the sugar is dissolved.
10. Have an adult carefully pour the hot sugar solution into the jar until it is full. Then put the paper clip and string into the sugar solution. Make sure the string hangs down in the middle of the jar.
11. This process took about 2 weeks to complete.

Conclusion

Observe as the sugar crystals grow for the next few weeks. When you combined the water and sugar you made a super-saturated solution. This means the water and the sugar stick together if both were very hot. As the water cools down, the sugar comes out of the solution back into sugar crystals on your string. The string together with the paper clip act as a "seed" around which the crystals start to grow. With some luck and patience you will have a tasty scientific activity Enjoy! You and your friends can now begin making tasty Candy Rock Crystals.

Enhance and develop your kids ability with fun-filled home-made science experiments.

Visit
BABY PROFESSOR
EDUCATION KIDS
www.BabyProfessorBooks.com
to download Free Baby Professor eBooks
and view our catalog of new and exciting
Children's Books